The Developing People Toolkit

For a complete list of Management Books 2000 titles
visit our web-site on http://www.mb2000.com

Other books in this series include:

The Communication Toolkit
The Customer Service Toolkit
The Human Resources Toolkit
The Learning Toolkit
The Motivation Toolkit
The Systems Thinking Toolkit
The Team Management Toolkit

The Developing People Toolkit

Practical ways to improve personal and work performance

Stuart Emmett

2000

This book is dedicated to my family – to my wife, the lovely Christine, to our two cute children, Jill and James, and James's wife, Mairead (also cute), and to our totally gorgeous three granddaughters, twins Megan and Molly and their younger sister, Niamh.

First published in 2008 by Management Books 2000 Ltd
Forge House, Limes Road
Kemble, Cirencester
Gloucestershire, GL7 6AD, UK
Tel: 0044 (0) 1285 771441
Fax: 0044 (0) 1285 771055
Email: info@mb2000.com
Web: www.mb2000.com

British Library Cataloguing in Publication Data is available

ISBN 9781852525651

Contents

About this book

In writing this book, I have made best-efforts endeavours not to include anything that, if used, would be injurious or cause financial loss to the user. The user is, however, strongly recommended, before applying or using any of the contents, to check and verify their own company policy/requirements. No liability will be accepted for the use of any of the contents.

It can also happen in a lifetime of learning and meeting people, that the original source of an idea or information has been forgotten. If I have actually omitted in this book to give anyone credit they are due, I do apologise and hope they will make contact so I can correct the omission in future editions.

About the author

My own journey to "today", whilst an individual one, did not happen, thankfully, without other peoples involvement. I smile when I remember so many helpful people. So to anyone who has ever had contact with me, then please be assured you will have contributed to my own learning, growing and developing.

After spending over 30 years in commercial private sector service industries, I entered the logistics and supply chain people development business. After nine years as a Director of Training, I then choose to become a freelance independent mentor/coach, trainer and consultant. This built on my past operational and strategic experience – gained in the UK and Nigeria – and my particular interest in the "people issues" of management processes.

Trading under the name of Learn and Change Limited, I currently enjoy working all over the UK and also on four other continents, principally in Africa and the Middle East, but also in the Far East and South America. In addition to my training activities, I am also involved in one-to-one coaching/mentoring, consulting, writing, assessing and examining for professional institutes' and university qualifications.

I can be contacted at stuart@learnandchange.com or by visiting www.learnandchange.com. I welcome any comments.

Preface

Welcome to this new series of business toolkits designed to improve personal and work performance.

A recent report entitled "The Missing Millions – how companies mismanage their most valuable resource" (source: www.Proudfootconsulting.com) stated that "Poor management in the UK is directly responsible for 60 lost working days per employee per year. And a further 25 days lost annually can also be indirectly attributed to management failing."

That is a total of 85 wasted days per employee every year due to poor and failing management. This is around 30% of a normal working year of 240 available days!

According to the report, the main contributing factors were as follows:

- Insufficient planning and control
- Inadequate supervision
- Poor morale
- Inappropriate people development
- IT related problems
- Ineffective communication

This series of concise guides will provide practical advice in each of these key management areas, to enable managers to get the most out of their teams, and make sure that they stay ahead of the game.

The simple truth is that in order to avoid the incredible 85 wasted days per employee per year referred to above, things must be done better *by management*.

Problems with management will almost always turn out to be people problems. Improving performance is therefore essentially about improving individual and team performance so that, in turn, the organisation's performance is improved.

This will require that, for example, the following are considered:

- Developing a strong strategic vision that is underpinned with learning
- Motivating and developing and releasing the potential of people, as individuals and in teams
- Communicating to people what is expected, what they are rewarded for, how they should deliver results and what results the organisation is looking for.

The earlier mentioned Proudfoot research highlighted several areas that managers can work on to improve performance. These are shown again below with a link to the appropriate Toolkit:

- Insufficient planning and control – see the Systems Thinking Toolkit
- Inadequate supervision – see the Team Management Toolkit
- Poor morale – see the Motivation Toolkit
- Inappropriate people development – dealt with in this Developing People Toolkit
- IT related problems – see the Systems Thinking Toolkit
- Ineffective communication – see the Communication Toolkit

It should be appreciated that many of these aspects do inter-relate, and that a single quick fix in one area may not always work very well. The Systems Thinking Toolkit does examine more fully all of the interconnected links of inputs, processes and outputs to be considered when improving performance. Also, the Learning Toolkit is paramount, as improvements can only be made after making changes and change, in turn, is directly associated to new learning.

As we have seen, many of the Proudfoot research aspects are directly people-related. In addition to the specific toolkits mentioned above, the Human Resources Toolkit provides a complete framework for effective human resources management.

Finally, as we all know, no business can survive without customers, and the essential skills of customer service are absolutely vital to the retention and growth of the customer base. The Customer Service Toolkit provides quick and easy advice which will produce startling returns.

Part 1. Development and Learning

Professional and personal development is important. Organisations need to create opportunities for different types of experiences and ensure people are nurtured. As people development involves moving people from one position to another, this means that learning will be needed; changing and learning are directly connected.

One of the difficulties with learning, however, is that many people think they can get along without it. They either think that their knowledge is sufficient already, or they believe that they will learn by experience without any conscious effort. Needless to say, this a dangerous view to hold in times of continual challenge, and new developments.

Learning is not a passive activity or an automatic process. It may seem to be a passive activity once you have learned something, but to learn anything actually requires an active approach. Learning involves activity, it needs thinking about, and it can be hard work. But if approached in the right way, and flexed to the needs of the individual, it can also be fun.

We have covered this topic fully in "The Learning Toolkit". For the purposes of this toolkit we will confine ourselves to a brief summary of the principles.

Definition of learning

We define learning as follows:

> Learning is the method and process which uses personal-power, knowledge and experience to:
>
> - make sense of things, (by thinking)
> - make things happen, (by doing)
> - bring about change, (by moving from one position to another)

Learning is our future

We should all be learning most of the time, so that we can keep up with all the ongoing changes and developments in the world and in business. The rate and speed of change is dramatic. Those who remain in the past can quickly have outdated knowledge and skills. Competence is not a constant. Development must be dynamic and not static. The only thing certain about the future is that it will be different, so learning is fundamental to our "tomorrow."

This is not to say that all change is good. But new developments do need to be examined. Often the best way to do something may eventually be the simplest way, but, only after it has been examined, thought about and applied, (i.e. it has been actively learnt).

> *In times of change, it is the learner who will inherit the future.*

Learning needs skills

Learning involves developing skills and competencies in response to both present and anticipated future challenges. Learning is not just about obtaining qualifications, but is fundamentally about doing things better and doing things differently.

Individuals can no longer systematically rely on others (such as employers) to sponsor and support their learning. Leaving such an important decision to someone else is dangerous. Remember that it is actually your development.

Any organisation will only develop and learn through its people. It is individuals who do the learning in companies. It is therefore the responsibility of individuals to promote their own learning.

Self-development is your unique and personal journey. Many opportunities are available to you. It is therefore important to learn how to manage your own development and to stop depending on others to do this for you. As a skilled learner, you will then be able to:

- Anticipate learning opportunities
- Recognise development situations
- Seek out new learning
- Take risks and innovate
- Seek help and feedback
- Use interpersonal competencies
- Be self-critical constructively
- Filter and make connections
- Overcome barriers to learning

> *Having the ability to learn, you will also have the abilities to survive and to succeed.*

We can and do learn anywhere and anytime. Learning activities can take place in many different situations. Learning is not just about courses and qualifications, but includes informal and formal situations such as the following:

Informal (or unstructured) learning, such as:

- work experience projects
- coaching and mentoring
- job rotation and work shadowing
- planned reading
- attendance at ILT meetings
- using multi-media resources

Formal (structured) learning, such as:

- attendance at courses, conferences and seminars
- distance learning with feedback or some form of assessment
- studying for a qualification
- undertaking research
- coaching and mentoring
- job rotation and work shadowing

Learning does not always have to directed towards an outcome that is upwards, such as a promotion; it can be about broadening your skills, knowledge and/or competence at all levels.

Learning can also result from making mistakes (assuming you do not keep repeating the mistake!).

Indeed, most of our learning comes from our own experiences and not from others' wishes or commands or dictates.

Learning is personal

Learning is a unique and personal process. It is not always a formal process. No two individuals have followed the same path to get them where they are today.

We do many things without thinking about them. This is what academics would call being unconsciously competent. But before we first learnt to perform that action, we were incompetent and our learning had to become a conscious process. Think about driving a car. After we have done it for a few years, we then drive without thinking about all the very many complex things we do – until perhaps we have a near miss, *then* we think about how we drive. Soon aferwards it becomes an automatic activity again, until the next "incident", and so on.

Do you remember when you *started* learning to drive? You drove slowly, missed gear changes, used kangaroo petrol, clipped corners, got frustrated, thought you would never be able to do it... Yet now you drive "unconsciously" for most of the time.

> *Learning needs to be a self-driven journey*

Driving is a useful analogy for how we learn. We never learnt to drive a car by reading a book or watching someone do it. Reading and watching may have been a part of the process, but to learn how to drive, we had to do it.

Learning needs doing

Learning experiences must therefore involve doing. A Chinese proverb states, "I hear and I forget; I see and I might remember; I do and I understand."

The "doing" is very important for learning. Being active is central to learning.

> *What we think about or what we believe in is, in the end, of little consequence. The only consequence is what we do.*

To help you on this "doing" you need to appreciate that learning is a cyclical process, as shown below:

- We start by gaining experience – we do something
- We then think about the experience and try to understand it – we reflect
- We then make a choice – we reconsider
- We then decide what to do next – we revise
- We then do something again

Learning is therefore cyclical – a never-ending spiralling process. Once one "project" ends, it leads onto other "projects".

Learning is also an active process. There is no self learning without your action. Learning and doing and changing are all interlinked and interconnected.

Learning involves you in all of the following:

Knowledge → Skills → Motivation → Doing

"I Know" → "I Can" → "I Will" → "I Do"

You will see that motivation is involved and this is covered fully in the Motivation Toolkit. Motivation is needed to get us to do something. Learning is always a decision of our "will". As the saying goes, "You can take a horse to water, but cannot make it drink." You can, for example, be sent on a training course, but whether you learn anything is very largely dependent upon you.

> *People learn because they want to, and when they see it is worthwhile.*

Learning will require your conscious effort. Learning how to learn is itself a skill to be developed. Continuing professional development (CPD) will help you with this skill – CPD will certainly make your learning a conscious process.

> *Learning to learn is often about making the unconscious conscious.*

Part 2. Individual Development and CPD

Continuing Professional Development (CPD) is defined variously as:

- "The systematic maintenance and improvement of knowledge, skills and competence throughout a professional's working life"

- "The process by which a professional person maintains the quality and relevance of professional services during their working life"

CPD is an individual's commitment to ensure that their knowledge and skills are maintained in a changing world, at a suitable level. CPD is about maintaining standards of competence and professionalism. It puts the emphasis on you, taking responsibility for developing and directing your own career. It involves the conscious updating of your professional knowledge and the improvement of your personal competence throughout your working life.

Many professional career development standards require that you are able to explain:

1. How wider environments affect your career
2. The relationship between your aspirations and the labour market
3. The external sources of support that are available
4. The role of outplacement and support
5. The importance of self-assessment
6. The differing and changing career needs
7. Mechanisms for evaluating career management

Always remember, it is *your* development and nobody else's. No-one will force you to do it. It is all about being committed to your own growth and your success and survival in a changing and developing world.

> ### If it is to be, then it's down to me

Why bother with CPD?

The world is developing and evolving at an ever increasing speed, and in a variety of different ways. The types of change that we need to deal with professionally include the following:

- Developments in technology
- New and shifting markets
- Changes in the economic situation
- Greater emphasis on community and the environment
- A more mobile international workforce
- Preparedness for a promotion or a change of job

All these changes place emphasis on the continuing need for an individual to be professionally competent.

Major professional institutes also have a responsibility to maintain standards and to ensure public and environmental safety. Employers, clients, and the public all require, better standards, faster and at a lower cost. CPD will help you to prepare for and cope with the challenges that will face you in the future world of work.

The time for self-development is always "now". The pace of change has never been so fast; we have never had access to as much freely available and high-quality learning as now. If we abdicate responsibility for managing our own development, then, for sure, we will be less valuable to those we want to work for in the future.

> **Learning is not compulsory; neither is survival.**

There are six stages of interest in professional self-development, starting from total inertia and moving through to a total commitment to improve. Which stage describes your current position?

- Level one. I have development needs, but I am not interested in them.
- Level two. I have development needs, but I do not know what they are.
- Level three. I have development needs and I know what they are, but I will not do anything about them, as it is not my responsibility.
- Level four. I have development needs and I know what they are, but I need a push to do anything about them.
- Level five. I know about my development needs and I want to do something about them, but I do not know how to start.
- Level six. I know about my development needs and I want to do something about them and I am doing something about them.

How to undertake CPD

Effective learning involves combining the two halves of learning: theoretical learning (knowing how) and practical learning (putting the theory into practice) – or, respectively, knowledge and competence. Both halves of learning are needed, as knowledge can become isolated without the applied competence.

CPD will involve recording both knowledge and competence. However, this is not the same as notching up points. Attendance on a course, for example, does not necessarily mean you have actually *learnt*. The test of learning comes in your application of what you have learnt.

Successful CPD schemes will therefore require that you will keep written records in two areas:

1) Your record of achievements

This is a full record of the learning action taken and the respective outcomes

2) Your development plan

This looks ahead and states your objectives, with the actions and plans to achieve these outcomes.

As learning is an individual process, this record keeping will naturally need to be individually based. This is your own route-map that will help you get from where you are now to where you want to be. It will help you become an active learner.

Learning is learnable

Getting started

Before you complete your route map, you will find it useful to consider the following key questions. (To help on this, you might find it useful to review your last work-based appraisal or development review.)

Starting Out Qestions

1. **Where am I now?**
   - What is my Current Position?
   - What is my current knowledge and competence?

2. **Where do I want to be, or where am I going? What is the Future Situation?**
   - What outcome do I want at this time?
   - What is the target I want to aim at?
   - What direction am I being moved towards?

3. **How am I going to get there?**
   - What is the gap between where I am now, and where I want to be?
   - What is the knowledge and competence required?
   - What actions do I need to take?
   - What resources do I need?
   - What support do I need?

4. **How do I know I have arrived?**
   - Are there any intermediate steps?
   - What are the criteria that will tell me I have arrived?
   - What are the criteria that will tell me I am at the end of this current stage?

These four questions can then be looked at in greater detail by using the following Steps 1-4.

Step 1 - Review

To start the review process, you should review your personal and professional experience. This will enable you to identify your interests and present level of skills and knowledge. Analysis of future needs will enable you to take account of current and future job and career requirements.

From this, you can draw up a profile of your personal and professional competencies and skills. This will help you to identify and prioritise areas for development.

Step 2 - Set your goals

To achieve your objectives you need to set specific targets. You may have medium or long-term goals, but it is best to concentrate on short-term ones that can be achieved in about 12 months. Many long-term goals can be broken down into a series of short-term ones. Balance your goals so that they include:

- Immediate job requirements
- Business and career aspirations
- Personal targets
- Family and personal considerations

Set yourself definite targets, in order of priority, that are practical, achievable and challenging. You will also need to set yourself realistic timescales, and establish criteria to help you evaluate outcomes.

Step 3 – Development activities

Identify the appropriate learning and development activities that will meet your needs. Think about all the available opportunities for development as well as any preferences and constraints.

To meet your development needs and achieve your targets you can choose from a wide variety of activities, both formal and informal. The choice of activity is up to you so long as it is part of your overall CPD plan.

Although most activities will be planned, you should also recognise and take advantage of other learning opportunities which may not be planned. These arise from day-to-day work experiences, unexpected challenges, and professional contacts.

Step 4 – Evaluate the outcomes

In order to assess the benefit of your CPD activities, their outcomes should be measured against the objectives that were set in Step 2. You should aim to evaluate your development in terms of new and/or improved levels of competent performance in your work, and new areas of knowledge acquired.

You will want to ask yourself four questions:

1. **Have I achieved my targets?**
   - Fully, partially, or not at all?
   - If not, why not?
   - If not yet achieved, do I need more time?

2. **What improvement can I see already as a result?**
   - Promotion or more responsibility?

- Increased confidence?
- Better working relationships?

3. **How else can I use the new skills and knowledge?**
   - Improving procedures/quality of service?
   - Developing a new project?
   - Coaching/mentoring colleagues?

4. **What am I going to do next?**
   - Continue with targets that need more time?
   - Work towards a higher level of competence?
   - Seek formal recognition/qualification?

In addition to this evaluation of your achievement against your targets, you should also reflect on the process: did the chosen method work for you? This will help you to decide which method to choose (or avoid) in future.

Having worked through these four steps, you are now well on the way to self-development. Ask yourself:

- How committed am I in progressing my CPD?
- Where am I currently limiting myself in progressing?
- What am I willing to risk so I can make outstanding progress?
- What have I recently succeeded in?
- What was special about what I did then?
- What evidence could I gather to show increased commitment to my CPD?

Finally, what should you do next? Some suggestions follow:

- Complete the following development planner.
- Get feedback on the plan from friends or colleagues.

- Above all, do not be like the person who said "I was going to read a copy of The Power of Positive Thinking, but then I thought, what good would that do?" So, do commit to doing something positive about your CPD!

Personal Development Planner

Stage 1. Preliminary

1. List, all your personal attributes, experiences and interests to obtain an honest picture of what you are what you want to be.

2. List all the possible areas for expanding your knowledge of a topic.

3. Compare 1 and 2.

4. Score each topic using a 1-5 scale for:
   - your interest
   - your ability
   - your potential scope for use

5. Pick the top three topics, and research each in depth, for example by
   - talking to someone
   - reading about them
   - searching the internet
   - watching appropriate TV programmes
   - attending self-training courses
   - going to exhibitions, conferences, seminars
   - phoning up and talking to people, with a "can you help me?" approach

Now move on to create your develop plan

Stage 2. The development plan

1. What do I want to achieve?

2. When am I going to do this?

3. How will I know it is successful?

4. Target Date

At the designated Target Date, move to Stage 3.

Stage 3. Progress review

1. What have I done?

2. What have I learnt?

Transfer to your Record of Achievements

Stage 4. What do I do next?

1.

2.

3.

Transfer to your next Development plan/.......................

You should always maintain a Record of your Achievements. If you do not this, then who else will? This record can start with keeping a copy of any acknowledgements of your progress (congratulatory emails, for example); these will act as a reference for others and a personal reminder for you.

Meanwhile, a formal record may contain the following:

- List of qualifications/competences, including details of awarding body (if appropriate) and date
- List of skills or competencies learnt at work, with details of where the learning occurred and when.
- List of skills or competencies learnt outside the workplace, with details of where the learning occurred and when. This learning would come from things like courses, professional institute meetings, discussions with colleagues, reading, film/radio/tv and so on.

Part 3. Helping People to Develop

As we have established, learning and development is not an automatic process, and whilst an individual's personal motivation is a key aspect, people will often need help and support in their learning.

This help and support process is known as "mentoring". However, the name used is secondary to the process involved – a process where organisations create opportunities for people to have different types of experiences and be nurtured (or "mentored") in their learning and developing at work.

Learning in the workplace

The myth exists in many organisations that the only way for anyone to learn anything is to send them on a training course. Learning, however, will not be confined to the training course sessions. Certainly, most trainers will "plant seeds" and will work very hard to ignite the fire for continued growth and development when the learner returns to their work environment.

However, there are some necessary conditions for learning and development to happen in the workplace. These involve the active support of managers who must, in effect, take responsibility for watering the planted seeds. If this does not happen, then applied learning opportunities will be missed and the training event time and cost will be wasted.

A person being developed needs the following from their managers:

- Identification of development needs
- A development programme
- A learning culture at work which fully understands:
  - how people learn
  - how to support/coach/mentor

This learning culture must include continuing support, both before and after a development programme – something which many companies find a real challenge.

Managers should be prepared to follow the following crucial steps in planning and implementing a development programme in the workplace:

1. Planning a development programme:
- Think what work-based projects can be used to apply learning and benefit the business.
- Ask the learners to seek feedback on their current performance so that they come up with specific learning goals in this work based area.
- Let them do a pre-task.
- Meet and finalise learning goals.
- Stimulate interest in the programme within the company.
- Put learners into learning sets/buddy groups.
- Arrange a mentoring scheme/programme(see below).

2. Delivering and monitoring the development programme:
- Ensure ongoing mentoring support
- Evaluate the success of the work-based project
- Ensure specific opportunities exist with 2 days of the end of the programme
- Discuss the learning with the employee
- Reinforce the learning by having the employee teach others

- Publicise the success of the programme
- Link rewards to the transfer of learning into the workplace
- Continue with successful learning groups by transforming them into improvement teams

Only in this way can the crucial transfer take place into the workplace and become effective applied learning that will work towards creating high-performing organisations.

Organisations who are able to deliver this kind of development support are likely to have the following characteristics:

- Opportunities for continuous learning
- Information sharing
- Employee participation
- Links between personal compensation and performance
- A flat organisation structures with cross-functional working
- A supportive work environment

Learning on the job

To be successful, the learner on the job must go through the following stages:

- Doing – being "active" and "practising"
- Reflecting on what has been done, by "thinking" about it
- Reconsidering the "theory", with particular regard to others' "best practice" or "facts"
- Revising the application, by considering what to do differently
- And then, putting the revised procedure into practice

As explained in the Learning Toolkit, effective learning conditions are as follows:

- Motivation – "what's in it for me" (WIIFM)
- Getting expected outcome (achieving WIIFM)
- Stimulating recall of existing knowledge/skills
- Developing new opportunities.
- Receiving feedback, e.g. .praise
- Appraising own performance
- Transferability of knowledge, e.g. work applications
- Review, retention, practice

Effective supporting of learning will therefore compliment the above, for example:

- Giving motivation
- Helping achievement and recall
- Providing new opportunities
- Giving feedback
- Praising performance

Supporting learning and behaviour change

All regular habitual behaviour patterns become hard-wired in the neural pathways of the brain. The behaviour pattern becomes automatic at the brain-cell level, with the end result that the behaviour now feels natural, easy and comfortable.

Introducing a new required behaviour can often be extremely difficult, because it means replacing the old pattern. Behaviour patterns have been physically established at the brain-cell level, so that any new pattern will seem extremely awkward – even if it makes sense and is desired.

The brain is not like a digital computer and there is no easy available "delete" key. The only way to replace an old behaviour pattern is to establish a new one that will prove to be more satisfying than the old behaviour. With an adequate period of reinforcement, new connections will be made, so that this new pathway can become the preferred wiring. Over time, the old habitual pathway will eventually fall into disuse.

However, without reinforcement, the pathways will not establish themselves. Then most people will fall back on the old, comfortable patterns they are used to.

The only thing that can create permanent behavioural change is frequent reinforcement over the long term. This means receiving support by ongoing feedback, guidance, praise and encouragement. This support can be internal (DIY) or external (from other) - preferably both.

The Learning supporter

Perhaps now at this stage, we should define what a learning supporter or mentor is:

> A **mentor** is a one-to-one personal adviser, of equal status, in a defined and agreed relationship, whose aim is to assist learning and to improve, personal and professional effectiveness."

A mentor is therefore someone who:

- Helps another person through a learning experience
- Gives help which can be informal (responding to a personal request for help), or formal (for example, within an organised company mentoring scheme)

- Gives one-to-one attention
- Is totally focussed on learning potential

The mentoring relationship must be non-political and non-judgemental. The mentor should be of equal status, and in this respect it is important that the mentor should not have any direct management responsibility over the individual concerned.

What mentoring is not

Mentoring is not a place to:

- moan or whinge
- spread gossip
- be told exactly what to do
- be given specific answers to problems
- be sloppy and slapdash
- forget that learning is an active and continual process
- be managed
- ignore things that need to be changed and done differently
- expect answers to everything

There are two people involved in a mentoring relationship; the mentor and the person being mentored, the learner (or "mentee"). The learner is there for personal gain, as the following checklist shows.

What is mentoring for the learner?

Mentoring is a mechanism for the learner to:

- self-develop
- be challenged
- recognise their strengths and weaknesses
- learn to build on their strengths
- receive feedback
- learn by example
- learn by mistakes
- talk openly
- receive wisdom and insights
- listen
- be listened to
- gain knowledge
- do things differently
- be supported
- be encouraged
- trust and discuss

Mentoring can cover a number of subjects, such as work issues, career development, personnel development, or domestic issues.

The importance of supporting learning in organisations is widely recognised. In a 2004 Survey "Motivation Matters" conducted by the Chartered Management Institute and Adecco, mentoring was rated twice in the top three most effective training techniques that had been experienced by managers. Top-ranked was informal mentoring; second was participation in seminars; and third was formal mentoring.

Benefits of Mentoring

To a Company
- Widening of the knowledge and skill base
- Alternative training device, complimenting other training
- Part of an individual's personal development programme
- Recognising the value of individuals
- Developing committed and motivated learners who contribute to the company's success
- Developing team approaches and future management
- Can develop company culture

To the Mentor
- Highlighting some of own learning gaps and areas for personal development
- Learning to listen and reflect
- Developing knowledge about other areas
- Improving leadership and communication skills
- Learning to challenge, and to balance give/take
- Increasing job satisfaction, for example, by helping others
- Passing on knowledge and skills to others, for example by giving something "back"
- Discovering different ways of working with people

To the Learner
- Developing learning and reflective skills, the keys to personal potential
- Developing personal as well as professional knowledge
- Learning to take risks in a supportive environment
- Learning to accept criticism
- Developing autonomy and accountability
- Increasing confidence and openness to change

Learning support activities

The provision of learning support involves a number of business process activities:

- Planning, for example determining what has to be done
- Recording, for example keeping minutes of meetings
- Structuring sessions into (i) review (ii) agenda and (iii) action points
- Time management, for example looking at all activities and prioritising
- Maintaining boundaries, for example around political issues
- Scheduling, for example planning in when to do things
- Evaluating, for example after analysing
- Action planning, for example what needs to be done and when
- Facilitating , for example "oiling" the "wheels"

Mentors' interpersonal skills

Successful mentors, or learning support providers, will need to develop the following interpersonal skills:

- Negotiating and influencing, for example in prioritising
- Listening, actively
- Giving feedback
- Intervening, for example being prescriptive, informative, or confronting
- Motivating and encouraging
- Coaching/teaching
- Reflecting
- Creating positive conflict
- Challenging honesty, openness and trust

- Not judging, patience, tolerance and calmness
- Non-prejudicial and "value-free" from hidden agendas, politics, etc.
- Empathetic (can "walk in your shoes")
- Able to deal with different types of thinkers and learners

Mentoring is perhaps 80 per cent a common process, and 20 per cent unique to a particular situation.

Unique features of a given mentoring situation would include the particular abilities, thought processes or behaviours of the learner, specific technical requirements of a particular job, or the particular learning requirements of the individual (who may, for example, only require help in one specific aspect of performance).

Much of mentoring is however, a common and structured process of learning by design, instead of learning by chance. Mentoring as a process has to be managed, like all other business processes, by planning, organising, co-ordinating and controlling. Without such a clear management role, mentoring relationships may dissolve into a "cosy" relationship, without any specific outcomes.

Learner's viewpoint

We will now look at some specific aspects for learners in deciding whether or not they need a mentor, and what skills they should, ideally, bring to a mentoring relationship.

Do I Need a Mentor?

Do I need to:

- See a clear direction and feel that I am on the right path?
- Get past blocking obstacles?
- Stop constantly feeling that I am under pressure?
- Be more self-assured in handling people?
- Hear a friendly and challenging supporting voice?
- Get confirmation that I am at least going along the right path?
- Find new ways in a fast-changing world?
- Find new ways to solve old problems?
- Demonstrate better that I can do more than I am currently doing?
- Get confidential advice if I am moving into a new area?
- Have consistent help to see me through challenges and change?

"Yes" answers indicate a mentor could be of assistance.

Characteristics of a Good Learner

- Willing to learn and develop
- Willing to participate
- Intelligent and able to learn quickly
- Ambitious and wants to "get on"
- Keen to succeed despite problems
- Committed to learning and personal development
- Able to make contacts
- Flexible and adaptable
- Self-aware
- Well organised
- Able to receive constructive feedback
- Wants to be mentored
- Accepts challenge and positive conflict
- Trusts the mentor
- Prepared to be open and honest
- Prepared to make mistakes and take risks
- An active learner and committed to their own development
- Knows their preferred style of learning
- Has a positive view of themselves
- Takes ownership of the learning and drives it forward
- Will do things they do not want to do, so that they will become what they want to be

Learning supporter's viewpoint

We will now look at what is needed to make a good mentor, and the conditions a company should seek to establish to support a successful mentoring scheme:

An Effective Mentor

An effective mentor is:

- An open communicator
- Committed to learning
- Willing to share positive and negative experiences
- Good at giving realistic and positive feedback
- Able to help people to recognise their strengths and development needs
- Able to challenge constructively, with positive conflict
- Objective and able to stand back from day-to-day issues and focus on implications and outcomes
- "Action-orientated" and encourages actions to follow discussion
- Able to work in an unstructured programme
- Able to contribute to an open, candid atmosphere which encourages confidence and trust
- Good at asking open-ended probing questions

Successful Mentoring Schemes

To enable a successful mentoring scheme to operate, companies should ensure that:

- Participation is by willing volunteers who wish to succeed and grow
- All participants recognise that individual needs and company needs can be both satisfied.
- An initial pilot scheme is run before rolling out the mentoring scheme
- Top management support is shown in action as well as by words
- Appropriate awareness-raising and marketing of the scheme to the whole organisation
- A co-ordinator is appointed to manage and "own" the programme
- There is a "no fault" opt-out clause
- All participants are made aware of the potential risks and problems
- All participants (mentors, learners, line managers and any others involved) have effective knowledge of the process
- All participants have a clear understanding of the learners' needs and requirements
- Training and support is provided for both mentors and learners
- Mentors are carefully selected and matched to learners
- The scheme is properly monitored and evaluated in relation to the defined objectives and anticipated outcomes, involving feedback from all involved

- Confidentiality is integral in the programme
- Appropriate time is allocated to undertake mentoring
- A time limit is set for the mentoring programme

Part 4. The Mentoring Process

There are three definable stages in the mentoring process or life-cycle:

- **Starting out** – initiation of the process, and orientation of the participants
- **Core stage** – involving the establishment of the relationship and the development of behavioural norms – this stage moves from "adolescent" phase which focuses on nurturing and dependency through to the "maturing" phase which sees the development of independence and autonomy
- **Ending stage** – termination or "divorce"

At the start, the learner is dependent in the mentor. The mentor starts out as a friendly supporter, and then moves into a more directive role, before finally the learner becomes more independent and autonomous.

The ultimate aim of mentoring is to have a learner who is "self-sufficient", and able to:

- Define personal objectives and see that support and development are interdependent
- Understand their own role and position in relation to others
- Know how to tackle problems, interpersonal conflicts and get constructive solutions
- Use the necessary knowledge and skills to do the job
- Be self-confident in their current ability and know what they still need to learn
- Seek advice and support, and remain open to further positive conflict, learning and change

Starting out

This is essentially a courtship stage where bonding, rapport and trust begin to be formed. It is also similar to the forming and norming stages in Team Building (see "The Team Building Toolkit). The learner is likely to be a little uncertain of what is required, so the mentor needs to give encouragement and provide a clear structure

The following two checklists will help both parties prepare for the first session.

Mentor's preparatory checklist

- Why have I become a mentor?
- What do I offer/ what do I want?
- What significant issues might arise?
- What do I feel strongly about?
- Which are the areas (1) in which I prefer my learner to 'match' me, (2) in which I am neutral, and (3) about which I would like us to be different?
- What about issues of trust and respect?
- What are my own personal thinking and working styles?
- How do they affect the way I interact with others?
- Where will we meet, and how much time will we have?
- What mutual contacts are we likely to have, and how might this help?
- What is my attitude towards self-development?
- Who mentored me, and what did I gain from it?
- Who else is involved in this process (e.g. senior management, learner's manager)?

> ## Learner's preparatory checklist
>
> - Why have I become a learner?
> - What do I offer/ what do I want?
> - What significant issues might arise?
> - What do I feel strongly about?
> - Which are the areas (1) in which I prefer my mentor to 'match' me, (2) in which I am neutral, and (3) about which I would like us to be different?
> - What about issues of trust and respect?
> - What are my own personal thinking and working styles?
> - How do they affect the way I interact with others?
> - What mentoring skills do I want my mentor to have?
> - Where will we meet and how much time will we have?
> - What mutual contacts are we likely to have, and how might this help?
> - What is my attitude towards self-development?
> - Who has mentored me before, and what did I gain?
> - Who else is involved in this process (e.g. senior management, learner's manager)?

Agenda for the first meeting

1. Introduction
- Agenda confirmation
- Share personal and professional information
- Establish each other's learning style preferences

2. Planning the relationship

- Discuss what both hope to get of the relationship
- Agree what is meant by confidentiality
- Set the ground-rules – for example, run thorough the above checklists on preparation and establishing rapport
- In work-based mentoring with an external mentor, the mentor can learn about the workplace context, and similarly the learner can learn about the external mentor's work context
- Discuss how the relationship will be reviewed and what to do if "problems" occur
- Discuss and agree the outcomes and what will be regarded as "success"
- Agree, at this first meeting, several dates forward for future meetings. (This fosters mutual commitment to the relationship. Dates maybe cancelled with appropriate notice, but a new date should be immediately arranged.)

3. Conclusion

- Review and summarise the meeting
- Agree actions points
- Confirm the next meeting (date ,time, venue, potential agenda)
- Write the meeting minutes

Core stage

This moves from the planning stage into the actual "doing" stage where actions are proposed, implemented and reviewed. There may be some brainstorming required before agreeing on the proposed actions, but the objective is to move from the "storming" to the "norming" as quickly as possible.

As the mentoring process develops, the learner is progressively moved from being initially dependent on the mentor towards increasing autonomy and independence. In the latter stages the mentor continues to provide support, but the nature of that support becomes increasingly passive or reactive, for example concentrating on auditing the learner's strengths and weaknesses, and helping the learner to make their own decisions through the use of listening and questioning skills (see the "Communication Toolkit" for more on these skills).

The transition from dependency to independence can be delicate and requires particular sensitivity on the part of the mentor.

Typical Agenda – Middle Stages

1. Introduction
- Agenda confirmation
- Review of last meeting

2. Main part of meeting
- Review of targets achieved/actions taken
- Feedback and discussion
- Targets to be achieved by next meeting and longer term

3. Conclusion
- Summary of session
- Agreement of details for next meeting – date, time, venue, potential agenda.

Continuous review of the relationship

Throughout this core stage, both parties should continuously review the mentoring relationship, and there should be at least one formal meeting, perhaps halfway through the process, to discuss the relationship. This meeting should address the points listed in the following summary checklist.

Checklist – Mid-session review

- Has a clear agreement been established?
- Is the content of the agreement still relevant?
- How well are we both getting on, at a personal level?
- Is the relationship a professional one?
- Are there any parallel activities taking place at the same time?
- Is there any conflicting process or activity?
- Is a clear outcome starting to emerge for the learner?
- Are new alternatives still being generated?
- Are ideas being turned into appropriate actions?
- Is the learner now increasing in their autonomy and independence?
- What stage is the relationship currently at?

As the mentoring relationship develops and the positive results of the process become evident, these questions should be extended to include the following:

- Is the learner more able to define personal objectives, network, and find out answers for themselves?
- Is the learner more able to apply knowledge and skills?
- Is the learner more open to challenge and positive conflict?
- Is the learner more able to tackle problems, interpersonal conflicts and get constructive solutions with positive compliance?
- Is the learner challenging the mentor with positive conflict?
- Is the learner more proactive and keen to take the initiative?
- Is the learner still eager to continue learning?

Ending stage

This stage represents the end or a divorce, with perhaps some attendant mourning. Whilst in the earlier stages in the relationship the learner was more dependent, they are now more independent. The mentoring process which started with the "forming" aspects of initial relationship development, has gone through the honeymoon period (or perhaps a storming period), developed and established the norms, before finally reaching a good performing level. Accordingly, the steps of forming, storming, norming, and performing, now come to the final stage, which may be called a mourning stage. This is because if the relationship has got this far, then it should have been found to be enjoyable and been mutually beneficial. It is now over and a sense of loss can ensue. It is important to acknowledge any such feelings, as well as, concluding any remaining "open" business.

Before parting ways, the mentor and the learner should conduct a closing review of the progress and the success of the mentoring relationship as follows:

End Session- Mutual Feedback

- Is the learner really confident and autonomous?
- Did we have a good rapport for most of the time?
- Were we able to challenge each other, with positive conflict?
- Was confidentiality maintained?
- Did we keep focused?
- Was there an appropriate balance between direction and support?
- How have we grown as a result of the relationship?
- What was specifically helpful?
- What was specifically unhelpful?
- What would we do differently next time?

Problems

Finally in this section on the mentoring process, we will consider what problems may arise in the relationship. These can also show the "pitfalls" to be avoided.

Potential mentoring Problems

- Mismatch of mentor and learner
- Mismatch of expectations, for example from unclear starting agreements
- Reluctant mentor/learner, for example with "forced" matching and pairing, and a lack of commitment from one or both
- Lack of openness and trust, for example no challenging and positive conflict
- Relationship not valued in the organisation
- Gender or culture mismatch, creating misunderstanding
- Emotional involvement "clouding" the issues
- Broken confidentiality, leading to mistrust
- Conflicting roles, for example if the mentor is also the line manager
- Obstruction from others, for example colleagues or partners
- Parameters/boundaries/details not agreed in advance
- Cancellation of agreed meetings because of insufficient time available, raising the question "are we serious about this relationship?"

Part 5. Mentoring Skills

For a successful mentoring relationship, the mentor needs the right environment and resources, and above all the right skills.

Before we look at the specific skills needed by the mentor, let us first consider the specific needs of the learner. In addition to the learning skills and the positive motivation described earlier in this book, these needs include the following:

- An atmosphere that is friendly and conducive to learning
- Comfortable surroundings, warm, well-lit and with appropriate background music (if any)
- Encouragement from the learner's colleagues, family and friends
- Support from the learner's manager
- An appropriate *method* of learning (perhaps in a separate teaching facility, perhaps on the job, or perhaps by some form of distance learning).

Mentors should do all they can to ensure that all the above needs are met before embarking on the mentoring process.

Mentoring skills – how good are you?

The following statements all describe required attributes of a good mentor. Read these statements carefully, and make a note of those that you need to work hardest upon.

Skills checklist

1. I listen to the whole issue before commenting.

2. I give advice but still expect the learner to make their own decisions.

3. I always find time to help.

4. I always question thoroughly to find the real issues.

5. I always give honest opinions.

6. I have a good range of networks and contacts that can be utilised appropriately.

7. I am not intimidating – I'm easy to approach at any time.

8. I know what I am talking about – I am good at my own job.

9. I look for the reality within which a learner works.

10. I always focus on learner needs during a mentoring session.

11. A learner who does not get the point quickly doesn't irritate me.

12. I am an optimist.

13. I am encouraging.

14. I am always well prepared in advance.

15. I am a positive role model in terms of my own achievements.

16. I can help a learner believe in their potential.

17. I am open to new ideas.

18. I know when to introduce options, which may not have been considered.

19. I can challenge assumptions skilfully.

20. I am a positive person.

21. I possess great patience.

22. I am interested in people.

23. I am an active listener.

24. I am non-judgemental.

25. I feel comfortable about having my views challenged.

26. I am enthusiastic about mentoring.

27. I am very knowledgeable about developmental issues.

28. I am tolerant.

29. I don't expect a learner to be like me.

30. I am prepared to learn with the learner.

31. I can give feedback skilfully.

32. I can allow a learner the freedom and confidence to make mistakes.

33. I see my learners as equals.

34. I have sound judgement.

35. I am able to distance myself and maintain objectivity.

36. I am keen to allow learners to make their own decisions.

37. I keep in regular contact with those I mentor.

38. I take an interest in the individual learner-I value their views and what they say.

39. I am able to probe beyond the superficial.

40. I can provide the space for a learner to express their feelings.

41. I can draw out a learner's ideas and I'm willing to use them.

42. I have a true passion for developing others, and I really believe in the value of development.

43. I can avoid the temptation to direct conversation back to myself and my issues and experiences.

44. I can challenge constructively and directly to get to the important aspect.

45. I won't just tell a learner what they want to hear.

46. I never appear keen to get a mentoring meeting over with and move on to the next thing.

47. I don't talk about my own achievements too much.

48. I have a genuine desire to empower.

49. I am responsive to my learner.

50. I always look for the positive in people.

(Source: Andrew. Gibbons@lineone.net on www.trainingzone.co.uk/toolkits)

Communication skills

Above all, mentors need excellent communication skills, (for a fuller coverage, please see the "The Communication Toolkit"). In particular, mentors need to adopt the following guidelines in the two crucial areas of challenging and providing constructive feedback.

Challenging

Go for the positives, and not, the negatives!

- **Positive conflict** is constructive as it enables new learning through an open disagreement and discussion of ideas. The outcome is either a full agreement about the other's position (there has been a "we" view and a "walking in each other's shoes"), or finding a new "third" position, through taking an emotionally detached and objective "helicopter view". All those involved believe they have gained something from the conflict process.

- **Negative conflict** is destructive as it inhibits new learning through creating personal tensions among people. The outcome is seen by each party in terms of their own position only. Those involved are usually divided, with one party feeling they have gained, and the other feeling they have lost.

- **Positive compliance** encourages challenge and positive conflict, and recognises that these are needed for effective learning and changing. People are actively involved in shaping the outcome from a mutual awareness and understanding of the differences in their positions. They can change their position in the process.

- **Negative compliance** encourages blind or forced agreement which hinders effective learning and changing. It discourages open challenge and positive conflict on any differences from the "status quo". One party remains uninvolved and keeps quiet with "unspoken disagreement". This gives a "false" agreement, which can encourage mistakes to be repeated. People will internally remain with their own position, even though this will not be externally expressed in their "false" agreement.

Giving and receiving feedback

Giving feedback:

- Concentrating on behaviour and not on personal traits/characteristics

- Imagine how you would feel if you were on the receiving end of your feedback

- Balance both positive and negative messages

- Don't avoid weaknesses but always balance them by emphasising strengths and directing attention towards the behaviour that the person can do something about

- Choose the appropriate tone and language

- Encourage people to take responsibility for their own development

- Check, at the end, for understanding, by asking them to repeat back or summarise the feedback given

- Then, and always, end on a positive note

Receiving feedback:

- Listen carefully without comment until the other party has finished speaking (avoid interrupting with explanation or defence)

- Try not to let feelings get in the way of using important information that is being offered

- If the feedback is vague, ambiguous or generalised, then ask the person giving it to be more specific – and ask for examples, if necessary, to check your understanding

- If the feedback is loaded in some way, do not immediately rise to the defensive or dissolve in dismay. Express your feelings about the statement by saying "I feel angry/upset/confused when you say that"

- Do not just swallow any criticism whole – look for consistent feedback from a number of people before you do. Take responsibility for which aspects of the feedback you will act on – it's your choice to change your behaviour

- Choose what you will do as a result of the feedback

- Thank the person giving the feedback – remember it is often very difficult to give feedback

Conclusion

In the introduction we highlighted several areas that managers can work on to improve productivity. These are shown again below with a link, (in brackets), to the appropriate Business Toolkit.

- Insufficient planning and control (see the Systems Thinking Toolkit)
- Inadequate supervision (see the Team Management Toolkit)
- Poor morale (see the Motivation Toolkit)
- Inappropriate people development (dealt with in this Developing People toolkit)
- IT related problems (included in the Systems Thinking Toolkit)
- Ineffective communication (see the Communication Toolkit)
- Poor Human Resources Management procedures (see the Human Resources Toolkit)
- Poor customer service (see the Customer Service Toolkit)
- Poor training/learning for specific skills and procedures (see the Learning Toolkit)

Readers are encouraged to take advantage of the complete list of toolkits, which complement each other to provide a comprehensive portfolio of concise pocket guides to improved personal and business performance.